# Make Money Online

## 15+ Proven Income Strategies to Earn You $1000+ a Month in 60 Days or Less

# Table of Contents

# Introduction

Congratulations on purchasing your personal copy of *Make Money Online: 15+ Proven Income Strategies to Earn You $1000+ a Month in 60 Days or Less.* Thank you for doing so.

The following chapters will discuss some of the many ways you can become financially independent and leave the job you hate to spend your life doing what you love. Throughout these 15+ strategies, you're sure to find at least a couple of ideas that click with you that you can get started on immediately. All it takes is a bit of hard work in the beginning, then you can sit back and watch the money roll in.

## This Book Has Something for Everyone:

This book will include passive income ideas for those who already run small or medium businesses, along with those who are starting completely from scratch. There will be something for everyone in this book, and 20 different ideas for generating a reliable passive income within just 60 days!

## Take Control of Your Life:

If you're ready to live a life you can be proud of, you've found the right book! By the end of this book, you'll have a huge head start. As stated, not everything in this book will click with you, but if you read carefully, you will find a few different methods you can get started with today to earn an income passively within just 60 days.

Passive income is a goal that so many people have in this modern day. Wouldn't you rather stop being a dreamer and become a doer? Now is the time. It's my hope that this book will inspire you to take action and make your dreams come true.

There are plenty of books on this subject on the market, so thanks again for choosing this one! Every effort was made to ensure it is full of as much useful information as possible. Please enjoy!

# Chapter 1
# Why Aim for Passive Income?

Most ideas for generating passive income either don't generate much money or take up a lot of your free time (meaning it isn't passive at all). So you're likely wondering, what makes passive income actually work for you? Is it the smart ideas such as making online courses, or writing articles? You've probably given thought to at least a few different options.

This book is here to bring you one big list of the passive income streams that you are most likely to succeed with, and fast. Having it all in one place will allow you to compare each idea and then decide what will work best for your lifestyle and goals. Let's start with a basic definition to make sure we're on the same page.

## What Does Passive Income Really Mean?

When we discuss passive income in this book, we are talking about what will happen after you've already done the hard work and put in the effort to make it happen. In other words, first you need to put your nose to the grindstone and put in the hours, whether it's writing a great e-book (which allows you to enjoy the passive results after the initial work) or making a smart investment. There are two main types of passive income:

1. **Asset-related Passive Income:** This occurs when you already have something to start making money with, like a property to rent out, or money to buy stocks with. This refers

to taking the money you already have and turning it into more.

2. **Idea-related Passive Income:** The second main category of passive income is idea-related, such as the example about writing the book we just discussed above. These streams of passive income are earned through hard work and sweat.

## Why Aim for Passive Income?

Your next question might be how to stay motivated to begin earning reliable passive income streams. The truth is that first you have to really want it. What better way to get to this mindset than to look over the best benefits that come along with meeting this goal?

- **More Time with Your Loved Ones:** As life goes on and you get older, you will likely begin to appreciate family and friends even more. This means that you're going to want to spend as much time with them as possible, rather than a bunch of time slaving away at a desk.

- **A Job You Care About:** To many people, a job they actually care about and get excited for sounds like a distant dream. But after putting in the initial work to get your passive income streams flowing, it's truly inspiring to watch what can happen!

- **Something to be Proud of:** It gets boring and tiring to have job after job of working for someone else. Wouldn't you rather be your own boss instead of having to answer to someone? Wouldn't you love to know that you can never get fired?

- **Setting Your Own Hours:** The beauty of passive income is you don't have to work except when you want to! Once you get your income streams flowing in, you will be taken care of and anything extra you want to do is your choice. You can make just enough to cover your essentials or decide to aim higher and earn more and more. The choice is yours.

- **Fewer Financial Worries:** Nobody likes financial worries. In fact, stress is a silent killer. When you take matters into your own hands and are your own boss with passive income, you will not have as many financial worries.

## Still Not Convinced that Passive Income is for you?

If you still aren't convinced that passive income is the path for you, all you need to do is keep reading to find out whether the ideas in this book will inspire you to take action. You may find your life path in the following pages! It's never too late to get started.

# Chapter 2
# Renting, Investing, and Outsourcing

It's no secret that someone who already has a lot of money can find methods for earning passive income, from new technology startup ideas, to angel investing, to real estate investing. When you already have a lot of money, you have far more opportunities and options. But, do you have to be rich to make money? Is there any other way? And what about the average person who also wants to earn money, create reliable passive income streams, and be free from financial worry without a ridiculous amount of work?

It's entirely possible to earn up to a thousand dollars (or more) with passive income strategies. Typically, a bunch of work is needed up front to get your business going and prepared to earn some profit. However, there are fortunately a few ways to start out with either no investment or a small investment. Let's look at a few of these now. We will then cover more later on in the book.

## Passive Income Strategy #1: Renting.

Renting something out that you have will require some work upfront, but can lead to a monthly income that is stable and reliable. The most common method for doing this is renting your home or a spare room on sites like Airbnb, but plenty of other items that you own can be rented out.

You could, for example, rent your bike out for a few days on sites like SpinLister. You could also use the website Just Park to earn passive income by letting people park in your driveway. This is especially helpful when there's a sporting event in town or when a neighbor nearby needs somewhere to park. For this section, we will focus on renting out your home.

Keep in mind that, at first, this won't be a passive process. Only once you have a reliable method down for renting can it be passive, especially if you decide to hire someone to help you out.

## Tips for Renting Your Apartment or Home Out:

A lot of people have considered renting their houses or apartments out. Perhaps they are hoping for some extra income to just waiting for the economy to get better. There are countless reasons to do this, but the plan may become difficult (and not be very passive) unless you know the ropes. Here are some guidelines for ensuring you're ready:

## Understand the Level of Responsibility:

You must first figure out whether becoming a landlord is something you want to do. Sure, there are plenty of benefits to doing this, such as deterring damage or vandalism to your empty home, tax breaks, and of course passive income. But becoming a landlord will take some work at first and won't always go perfectly. You will have to:

- Be prepared for maintenance and repairs.

- Be ready to collect rent every month.

- Pay more for home insurance.

- Make your home appealing for renters.

## Get Your Home Ready:

When the market is down, you can't rent your house the way it already is. Tenants can be really choosy and attentive when picking a house when the market is down, because there is a higher availability.

- You can get ready for a tenant by cleaning the house thoroughly and ensuring that the appliances inside it are in great condition.

- If you've ensured that you'd rather rent an area or room out of your house, ensure that it's secured from the rest of the house.

## Know Which Terms to Use:

As soon as you've cleaned the house, make a list that includes the appealing factors of the place. Write down the features that are usually desirable, such as a garage, air conditioner, washer and dryer, and more. Use the right terms to make the property seem appealing, such as "stainless steel products," "maple wood," "high ceilings," or "hardwood floors."

## Post an Ad:

Once your place is ready, it's time to post an ad on a reputable and reliable website. You may also post it in your local paper, but these days, most people will look online for listings. In addition, keep in mind which time of the year you'll be renting. Typically, renters move into places during certain times of year. Studies show that during these seasons, you can get more for the rent on your unit. The warmer months appear to be the most popular, but make sure you look up which times are best for your city.

## Hire Some Help:

Becoming a renter can seem simple on the surface, but it's crucial to speak with professionals (such as an attorney) to ensure that you are following both the local property and tax laws.

## Price it Competitively:

Decide on what to rent your place out for by finding out the cost of other rental properties in your community and neighborhood. Keep in mind that potential tenants are going to be looking for the best deal, so price your place competitively.

## Have a Reliable Screening Process:

Once your house or apartment is ready to put on the market, start searching for the right tenant. Once you start this process, make sure the tenant is chosen very carefully. They must be able to pay rent on a timely basis and also take care of your home.

Here are some steps for ensuring that this screening process goes smoothly:

- Check for both references and credit histories to ensure that the potential tenant will be reliable and responsible.

- Request a security deposit from the tenant so that, when they move out, if anything is broken it's covered.

- Set a payment schedule that works for both you and the tenant.

As you can see, renting out your home can be great for both you and the tenant, but first you have to make sure you cover all of the steps and precautions listed above.

## Passive Income Strategy #2: Find Unique Real Estate to Invest in.

As mentioned before, renting your home out can give you a passive income stream, but it can require money to get going with, due to maintenance, mortgage, and fees for property management. Although this is a good start, you may take this to the next level by crowd sourcing investing in real estate. You can, for instance, use RealtyMogul.com and invest in property while another person handles the upkeep, sanitation, and other considerations. This is one way to invest in real estate on a commercial basis without having a lot of money to start with.

If you are considering investments for real estate, you will probably hope to earn money based on how much risk you're engaging in, while not having to spend a lot of time tending to the place. To make this happen, you need to be smart about the initial choices when making your purchase. Here are the criteria to meet to make sure this goes smoothly:

- **Make Sure It Pays a Quality Return:** When you purchase a house or apartment, you're using money from liquid assets, such as CDs, bonds, or stocks, and putting it into something that is not liquid at all; real estate. Make sure you are buying cash-positive homes that will bring you in great returns.

- **Aim for Low Risk:** Basically all real estate investment comes along with high risks. With these types of investments, it's always possible you won't see any profit, because many issues can pop up. If you are aiming to buy some real estate, try to get a fee simple title in either an entity owned by you or your name.

- **Make Sure It Isn't Time Consuming:** We are taking about passive income here, so finding something that won't require a lot of time to manage is ideal. Some houses will call for too much management, defeating the purpose of trying to make it a passive income source. Simple, basic properties that you rent with long leases to responsible tenants will be the least amount of work for you. Stay on good terms with the tenant to reduce issues in the future that could eat up more of your time.

## Passive Income Strategy #3: Start and Outsource a Microbusiness.

Entrepreneurs commonly come up with a lot of ideas but don't have enough time to follow through on them. Get started with a straightforward, simple microbusiness, such as making websites for doctors or content marketing. As soon as you've gotten started with this, and some faithful clients coming in, just outsource the business, including writing and project management.

There are plenty of websites that allow you to find virtual employees to help run your business. This allows you to earn your money passively. Here are some guidelines for doing this right.

## The Outsourcing Guidelines:

Owners of small businesses are great at achieving their goals, but as they take on more and more tasks, it's hard to make sure that each of these tasks are given enough attention. This is one of the many reasons why outsourcing is becoming so popular, to both save time, and earn more passive income. So, which tasks should you outsource?

- **Front Desk Work:** Choosing to hire an in-person front desk receptionist can be a bit costly. This is why a lot of business owners choose to outsource this position with sites like Conversational, rather than hiring someone in person. The duties you'd be outsourcing include scheduling, managing appointments, customer service, delivering messages, and answering phone calls. These duties would be taken care of remotely by your virtual receptionist, at just a fraction of the amount of money an in-person front desk worker would cost.

- **Design Duties:** Design duties are a crucial aspect of marketing and presenting your business to those who encounter it. To hire a full-time designer (graphic designer), however, is costly. This is because the job is often difficult and highly skilled, so outsourcing can be a great way to save money while still getting the design work you need done. Head over to sites like Fiver or DesignCrowd to outsource the graphic design work you need done.

- **Bookkeeping:** This is a job that is commonly outsourced. When your business gets bigger, keeping your books in order gets complicated and time consuming. This increasing complication calls for the skills of an experienced accountant. You can use Quicken, which offers software to help you keep track of your business's tax information and finances. The software will allow you to stay in control while offering you information about profits, expenses, bills, and more.

## Avoid These Mistakes with Outsourcing:

There are quite a few risks or challenges that can come up when you decide to begin outsourcing. Make sure you stick to these rules and guidelines to avoid these mistakes with outsourcing.

## 1. Don't Choose the First Candidate Available:

When you search for a reliable candidate for the outsourced position you want to fill, you will see no shortage of search results, but the first ones to appear are usually either put there by strategic key words or paid advertising. Rather than choosing one of those, do some homework to find a suitable candidate.

## 2. Don't Go for the Cheapest Choice:

Providers of cheap outsourcing are usually not very great providers. Don't go for cheap services, instead, look for cost effective work, otherwise you might have to deal with bad quality.

## 3. Don't Outsource A Lot Too Soon:

It can be exciting to start using an outsourced employee, but don't fall into the trap of outsourcing everything immediately. Rather, begin slow and add tasks as you go, to make sure your provider is comfortable and can handle more.

## 4. Don't Micromanage Your Provider:

Lastly, micromanaging your new outsourced employee is a mistake that a lot of business owners will make. Ensure that you make a good choice, so you don't have to worry about whether the provider can work independently.

## Passive Income Strategy #4: The Silent Partner Idea.

It's not necessary to have millions lying around to be an angel investor if you choose to be a silent partner for a growing business. Silent partners will invest some money into a company and earn healthy profits with not a lot of work required after setup. Choosing to take this role on will require serious study and research into the business, their service or product, and who their leader is. As soon as you feel okay with that startup's potential, choosing to invest can lead to passive income. This happens without the need for long hours of work and offers you freedom to strengthen your portfolio.

## What Does Silent Partner Mean?

A lot of business-savvy people have thought about being a silent partner. The idea of investing money into a promising company and enjoying the resulting profits without extra work is very appealing. Essentially, silent partners are people who invest money into companies and get some of the losses or profits of that company.

A silent partner isn't meant to have any responsibilities in the daily tasks of the company, which is why the word silent is used here. But they will have a say in matters that impact the company's management, since this will determine results that impact the silent partner.

## Silent Partnership Benefits:

There are quite a few benefits that a silent partner can enjoy that other business members cannot. For one, a silent partner doesn't have much responsibility for the daily goings on of the business. They are part of the operation due to their finances, not because of operations knowledge.

- **Investment Knowledge Isn't Needed:** You don't have to have detailed investment knowledge to be a silent partner for a company. Ideally, you should use due diligence to examine the history of the business, along with their potential for the future and profit/loss information. One common reason for individuals to want to become silent partners is the passive income stream that comes from it without much need to monitor their investment.

- **Trust is Needed:** The most important aspect to becoming a silent partner is being able to trust the group or person that is in charge of the company. As soon as this trust is established, you don't have many other responsibilities other than enjoying what you earn.

- **There is Always Risk:** Keep in mind that silent partnerships don't always go well, even if you have done all your homework. Even amazing companies will encounter unforeseen troubles. If this happens, you might be tempted to overreact and try to get involved with the management to fix the situation. But keep in mind that this would probably be stepping over your boundaries and causing problems.

- **You Need a Partnership Agreement:** You shouldn't skip out on this if you decide to become a silent partner. Come up with some strict limits for involvement in this agreement. You should also come up with an exit strategy in case the partnership goes wrong and you wish to get out of it. If everyone involved knows about these boundaries before the agreement is set in stone, you can avoid a lot of trouble.

As you can see, choosing to be a silent partner is a great opportunity if the right circumstances come along. Make sure you do plenty of research on the company, including their management staff, business records, and company philosophy, and this strategy for investing can be both lucrative and safe as a passive income method.

Businesses that have proven positive results might be hard to get into, since they don't always need financing from the outside, but if you come upon this opportunity, be decisive. This is not a passive income strategy that works for everybody, but it could work for you.

## Passive Income Strategy #5: Using CD Ladders to Earn.

People commonly invest in bonds and stocks to build up streams of passive income, but if you're an amateur investor, that isn't always a very safe bet. Consulting a financial advisor is one thing for planning your future and retirement, but building up passive income by yourself with investments is risky. If you aren't ready for that step, think about trying CD ladders, first. True, they have low rates of interest, but a CD ladder can help you secure a safe return and save money with what you invest.

This method relies on dividing your money into identical amounts, using CDs with varying dates of maturity. This, in turn, can intensity your return to receive higher amounts of interest income in the future. CDs (Certificates of Deposit) will offer you an easy and simple trade-off. This includes a higher rate of interest than a typical savings account, traded for leaving your money in the bank for a period of time. If this strategy is used the right way, with a CD ladder for instance, this can be maneuvered to pay off for you.

## What are CD Ladders?

The technique of CD laddering refers to using a group of CDs with various dates of maturity. These dates of maturity are spaced out similar to ladder rungs, over time. This technique lets you get higher yields from the long term CDs and protect yourself against possible disadvantages of keeping your money locked up for a long period of time. This technique may be applied in many ways and can be adapted to your situation for investing and saving.

## Why Should You Build One?

With a longer term CD, you get a higher interest rate. Committing to this will let you earn a higher rate of interest than just keeping money in your savings, which makes it easy to access. These types of CDs earn higher rates of interest than accounts such as money market accounts, as well.

- **CD Deposits are Covered by FDIC Insurance:** The FDIC (Federal Deposit Insurance Corporation) offers protection on CD deposits. In the case of your bank failing, your CD account is covered by FDIC and gives the money you had in it back to you.

- **They are Low Risk:** For those who wish to lower their risks in investing, CDs are a common and popular choice. In comparison with stocks, they have lower rates of return, since the current environment of low rates of interest. However, they aren't as risky and don't require a lot of effort for you as the investor. You won't need to keep an eye on the stock market if you go with CDs.

## CD Ladders, What are the Disadvantages?

Deciding to go with CD accounts does come along with two possible disadvantages. Here is a brief look into those, so you can be aware of them.

- **The Liquidity Problem:** With a CD account, you won't have any liquidity or access to the cash if you end up needing it.

- **Missing Hikes in Interest Rates:** Since CDs don't have any liquidity, that means you can't switch over to products that are higher yielding in the case of interest rates going up.

When it comes to CD laddering, you aren't obligated to be locked into just a single CD for a specific period of time. Rather, you are putting your capital into a group of CDs that have varying dates of maturity. This allows you to have access to your money on a regular basis, offering you liquidity in a predictable schedule, in order to adapt to higher rates of interest or to meet your own financial needs.

## Setting up Your First CD Ladder:

If you have an amount of $10,000 to deposit, you may place this into your savings account. However, if you don't think you will need access to it any time soon, a CD will allow you to earn more with that amount. But you may not wish to commit all of this money to a CD for five years, in the case of rising interest rates or an emergency that requires cash. In this circumstance, you would be better off using that money for a CD ladder. Setting up a simple CD ladder isn't hard. CDs last for varying lengths. Here are the steps for setting one up:

- **Figure Out the Amount to Put In It:** First, you need to choose the amount that you will deposit into your CD accounts to create the ladder. Remember that most banks have a minimum requirement of deposit for these in order to earn the APY (advertised annual percentage yield). The amount required to earn this could be anywhere from $2 to $25,000, or sometimes even more.

- **Choose the Lengths for Your CD Terms:** Your money being kept in the CD is going to earn you more interest automatically, but this is only possible if you don't withdraw any cash from the CD before its maturity date. Make sure you know both how long the length of your term is and also which penalties will occur if you withdraw cash before the CD's maturity date. CD term lengths include a single month, 2 months, 3 months, half a year, 9 months, 12 months, a year and a half, two years, two and a half years, 3 years, 4 years, or 5 years.

- **Choose the Division of Your Money:** Next, you must decide how you will divide your capital up to make the CD ladder. If your $10,000 is spread out in five CDs, each having $2,000, your money could be put into a 5-year, 4-year, 3-year, 2-year, and 1-year CD. This would allow you to enjoy liquidity every year, while still having your cash in long term, higher-earning CDs.

- **Reinvesting:** If this ladder is adjusted over time, it's possible to get more money out of it without sacrificing your yearly liquidity. Imagine that you purchased the five CDs mentioned, at the start of the year 2016. Once your single year CD was due as the year ended, you could just reinvest that for another year. But the first 2-year CD that was invested in would be due at the same time as that one. Choosing to roll your CDs over at the time that you originally chose would not allow your liquidity to come regularly anymore, resulting in this type of duplication.

- **Know the Fees:** It's true that a CD ladder helps you benefit from high rates and varying dates of maturity, but you should know about the fees that come along with this. Make sure you go over the fine print carefully and stay aware of any potential withdrawal penalties and the exact dates of maturity.

## You Could Lose Interest with Penalties:

As a consequence for withdrawing your money early before the date of maturity, you might have to suffer penalties, including losing out on your earned interest. Fees for early withdrawal are usually more severe when it comes to longer term CDs, rather than the shorter ones. Before you even consider using a CD ladder, look at the penalties for early withdrawal versus the CD rates interest. This will help you be aware of whether you should decide to be able to do early withdrawals or leave it alone until its maturity date.

## Think About More than One Bank Account:

For those of you who have been banking with the same branch for a long time, you should look into other choices for your CD ladder in order to receive the best benefits and rates. Maybe there's a bank that offers better CD rates. Look at MoneyRates.com to find the best deal.

## Reverse CD Ladders:

Reverse CD ladders are different from the basic type and involve CDs that have one single date of maturity, but are not purchased all at the same time. You may want to use this approach if you have something specific you're saving for, like a house payment. This will let you put some cash into the CD for some time, earn profits with the high rates of interest, then buy another one later on in order to keep your savings growing.

## How to Refine the Ladder:

Your CD ladder can be refined in a few different ways. You may heavily distribute the deposits to certain dates of maturity, more than others, in accordance with when you plan to use that money. You may also weight your cash more toward shorter CDs in the case that you believe the rates of interest will go up. Having a CD ladder helps you benefit from the high yields of long term CDs, and by spacing the dates of maturity out so they come regularly, you will have some liquidity. It does require some effort to get started with (as all other passive income streams do), but you might discover that it's worth your time and effort.

## Passive Income Strategy #6: Sell Your Personal Expertise.

A lot of people dismiss their own expertise as something ordinary that isn't worth much. However, that's not true at all. You can use your professional experience to run a team remotely or speak at a conference or seminar. Whether you know how to write, run a small business, or do bookkeeping, there are people who want to hear from you. Simply ask the audience members to get on your email list and make videos, create a book, or come up with a product for those who are interested in your expertise. Although this technique isn't completely passive (at first), the possibility of creating a product to sell to thousands is going to bring money in for a while, if you enjoy success.

## Passive Income Strategy #7: Rework and Repurpose What You Have.

What do you have in old computer files, audio notes, PowerPoint presentations, sample contracts, or business sheets? These can all be reworked and repurposed to be sold. Begin big, for example selling an entire series of resources for great business to your customers, and also try to sell Kindle books for paid members. Publishing content takes a lot of time and hard work. A lot of this work can be wasted if you only publish it on a single site, share it in a small area, and don't do much in addition to that.

Everyone is missing out on opportunity to rework the stuff they already created. There are countless ways to repurpose your content to make your brand stronger and more appealing to potential clients. These methods include using your email list, making your social profile farther reaching, and earning more passive income. This post will go over some methods for using the content you already have to create more, marketable content.

## Is This the Same as Copy Pasting?

Repurposing content was once as simple as copy pasting something you've already made to a different place, like a blog or article directory. But then Google realized what people were doing and used software to spin articles, which created "unique" writing by using an article that's been already published and using other synonyms for some words, so that Google didn't recognize that it was the same article. So Google realized that this is happening and it isn't recommended. It's better to use your time on something that gives value to others, not just to try to game the existing system.

That being said, some people won't feel okay with using content to repurpose it in another place. However, to me, this is fine. People absorb what they read in very different ways. If your good content isn't repurposed, a lot of people will miss out on listening to, watching, or reading it. This is a smart method for getting your work out there on a wider basis.

## Beginning with a Simple Post on Your Blog:

One very common content type is blog posts, so we will begin there. Is it possible to take some of your content and make it new? Let's look this over.

- Write your post and make sure it's been edited.

- Read the post aloud as you record your voice.

- Publish this as Sound Cloud content or a podcast episode.

Many people have both a blog and a podcast with exclusive content. You can read your blog posts aloud and sell them as audio blogs. This can increase your number of downloads and give some members unique content that they wouldn't have found otherwise. A lot of people prefer to listen to content rather than read it, so this can be a way to serve those potential customers in a unique way.

## Using Infographics with Your Work:

Here's another idea for taking your blog content to the next level. Just follow these simple steps:

- Create a post on your blog.

- Go over important points with a visual representation.

- Publish this as a shareable photo, a lead magnet, or a bonus.

Infographics are popular on social media platforms and can bring more traffic to your original blog post. They add value to both readers and the creators of the content itself. Most social media feeds are very visual, so this is a good way to make something that fits what is already popular. Do some research into how to create visually appealing and compelling work that is highly shareable.

## Making Memes with Quotes from the Blog Post:

This is a bit simpler than making an infographic picture that is meant to sum up your whole post, and involves just using a small portion of it. Here are the steps to get started with this idea:

- Create your blog post.

- Choose a few small quotes from it.

- Make this into a graphic using a tool such as Canva.

- Post this photo on Facebook or Instagram with a link to your blog.

This step is simple and highly effective. Many users online are visually focused, so having a nice picture to go along with it can be great for drawing traffic to your blog, thus raising your monthly passive income. Here's another idea to use.

## Making a Presentation on Slide Share:

This is another simple method for driving more traffic to your blog and finding more users to visit it.

- Create your valuable blog post.

- Make slides using visual and talking points from the blog post.

- Put this on the site SlideShare.net.

If your posts have visuals and are well-crafted, this won't take a lot of work to convert them over to SlideShare.net.

## Make a Live Stream with Your Content:

For this one, you can create a new style of content with what you already have. Just follow these steps to get started:

- Create your blog post.

- Use a live streaming platform like Facebook Live or Blab.

- Start a talk and use your blog post to come up with talking points while interacting with people. You can highlight some calls of action during this time to get people to buy your product or visit your blog.

You may record this video to put on YouTube or other places online to reach an even wider audience. At times, one post won't be sufficient to cover a whole topic, so you can make a series with two or three posts published in a row. This does require more effort but it will result in a more valuable product for your audience or customers. There are many other ways you can repurpose your existing work, such as…

## Making a Book from Your Blog:

If you have a specific series of blog posts on your blog about a specific topic, this can be turned into a book to sell! Here are the steps for doing that:

- Gather your blog posts or write them.

- Make each post a chapter in the book you're going to create.

- This book can be sold, given away as a prize or bonus, or used as an incentive for a signup to your email list.

A lot of bloggers out there have done this exact thing with great success. This can be a great way to kick start your journey of passive income.

## Passive Income Strategy #8: Selling Artwork Online.

The next passive income strategy we have on our list is selling digital artwork. There are countless options for doing just this, outside of only WordPress and stock photos. You can use Etsy to sell downloads of wallpapers, illustrations, graphics, and more to turn a profit. You can find so many stories online of artists selling their photos on social media. Use websites such as Candidly to connect photographers on Instagram with businesses who are seeking candid pictures for their ad campaigns. To do this, you first have to have a quality digital camera for photos.

# Chapter 3
# Using Apps for Earning Passive Income

Earning income passively with apps on your cell phone is one great way to improve your flow of side money. These don't need a lot of time or effort to get started with and as soon as you install the apps, you just have to cash out.

## Passive Income Strategy #9: Smart Phone Apps.

Each of these apps individually won't earn you a ton of money, but in addition to the other strategies in this book, they will help line your wallet a bit more and give you some extra cash over time. But how are you to know which to choose?

## Apps for Passive Income- What to Look for:

Before we get to our list of apps for passive income, you should consider the following when choosing which ones to start using. Here are the rules for choosing the right apps:

1. **Don't Ever Pay for It:** If you find an app that claims to give you free money but first asks for your card info, it's probably just a scam. The apps we will list in this chapter are completely free.

2. **Make Sure it's Easy to Setup:** Apps for passive income are supposed to be easy to put on your smart phone. If you look through the app and it seems like a lot of extra work to do, it likely will be. The idea is *passive* income, not active income.

3. **Ensure it's Low Maintenance:** Apart from getting it setup initially, you shouldn't have to do a lot of work to keep the app maintained on your phone. The majority of the apps we are about to discuss are just there in the background.

4. **Registration Bonuses:** It's recommended that you install a lot of apps for passive income since this will let you earn more, ultimately. Look for the ones that give you a sign-up bonus.

## The Best Apps for Earning Passive Income:

If you install the following apps on your smart phone or tablet, you will earn extra money within a short time. Remember that it all adds up after a while.

## Nielsen Consumer Panel:

This company, which was once known as Nielsen Digital Voice, is first on our list even though it doesn't pay better than the others. This is because the app can be installed on more than one device. Keeping that fact in mind, you may triple or double that money you have coming in. This app will pay you to be able to gather information about your smart phone, including the number of messages you send a day, which browser you have, and more.

This app is available for mobile devices, tablet, and desktop computers, but what you will make from it will depend on the device used. If you wish to put it on your desktop computer, you will only get free sweepstakes entries that offer cash prizes. So, if you can, try to put this app on your smart phone or tablet first and you will earn some money each month.

## Digital Reflection Panel:

Although it's not technically an app, you need to register your device to be a part of the program. But this program deserves to be on our list anyway. The Digital Reflection Panel functions by adding an internet meter to your existing internet router. Setup for this program requires just five minutes or so and there's a tech team there to help you if needed.

To find out whether you are eligible for the program, you have to take a small and easy survey, but you must answer honestly to get accepted. As soon as you install this and get your device registered, you will receive a bonus of $50, but only a month after completing a set of steps.

## Smart Panel:

This app begins by gifting you a bonus of $5 when you sign up. It's available on Windows, Android, iOS, and collects information in terms of how long you are on your device at a time and which apps are installed on it. This data is then used by them to make the internet better for users. To find out whether you are eligible to be a part of this program, you have to first take a small survey. You should qualify as long as you have some kind of smart phone. You will earn higher bonuses the longer the app is on your device. You need to wait at least a month in order to get some money from the app.

## Shop Tracker:

This app is great because you get a bonus of $3 automatically when you sign up for your account. This app works in a different way than the apps discussed in this section. Rather than getting money for giving information about the way your device is used, you will be paid to have your purchases on Amazon tracked. Shop Tracker is connected with a popular survey website called the Harris Poll Online company. Just connect your account on Amazon to this app and the work is done. It requires roughly 10 minutes to set up. Each month, you have to take a survey about your shopping experience on Amazon, which will only require a few minutes.

## Mobile Performance Meter:

This program will give you money in exchange for you allowing them to track your device usage. The app pays you money to gather information about your speed of internet, the number of messages you send, and the apps installed on your phone. This app can be run on various accounts but you can only have one smart phone with each account. You can only use this all on Android devices, at the moment.

## Savvy Connect:

This app is a program for generating passive income that is inspired by the site Survey Savvy. The app collects data about your shopping habits, the apps you use on your phone, and how you entertain yourself with your device. Every month that the app is installed on your device, you earn some money. You can have this app installed on up to three different devices, including mobile, tablet, and desktop. Once you're a member of this site, you get invites to high-paying, exclusive surveys which get sent to your email after you have completed your profile.

To earn even more on Savvy Connect, be sure to tell your friends about it, which gives you bonuses between $5 and $15. The only downsides with this app is that you have to receive payment by check and the software cannot be installed on your MacBook computer.

## Cross Media Panel:

This app pays you specifically for gathering data in your phone's browser. They will look at the site types you look at as well as how frequently you do this. By consenting to the gathering of this info, sites like YouTube, Android, and Google Chrome become more efficient and tailored for user's needs. You get a small bonus for registering your phone and then can receive weekly money and monthly amounts. You may cash out as soon as your account gets to at least $5 and you can choose which gift card you want.

Cross Media Panel works on your desktop computer, as well. Rather than putting their app on your phone, you may install their extension for your browser, but remember that you need to be using Google Chrome for this to work.

## MobileXpression:

To sign up for this app, you have to do it from a mobile phone or device. Once you have signed up you get a gift card for Amazon in just a few weeks after getting a membership. Although you don't earn a huge amount with this app, it's still worth it to have it because it's so simple to put on your device. Apart from making money in a passive way, you will receive some tokens that may be used for entering sweepstakes. They aren't easy to win, but they're free to try so worth signing up for. Remember that this program requires that you put a VPN on the phone you're using.

## Media Insiders Panel:

This app will track the types of advertisements you see, the websites you go to, and your activity on different social media platforms. The app works with Kindle Fire devices, iOS, and Android. This can be installed on up to three different devices to earn some passive money. When you install this program, you may have to wait two days before you see any account verification. To know that it worked, check for a green check mark near the app's mobile meter. You may earn even more passive income by using the app's included VPN. But this might have an impact on other passive income apps installed on your device, so make sure you check this and ensure it's okay.

## Data Coup:

This program isn't a mobile app, technically, so you won't have to do any installations to make use of it. Rather, you will just link your accounts on social media up to the website to earn some passive money for the data they collect from you. You may increase the amount you earn even more if you connect data like your credit cards and bank account. This doesn't sound safe on the surface, but the app doesn't have a way to find your credit card or bank account numbers, so don't worry. The app will only have the information related to the purchases made by you.

## Panel App:

This app shouldn't be confused with another app called Smart Panel app, which we discussed earlier in this chapter. You won't earn much with this application, but it's the easiest one on our list and does add to your overall monthly income stream. Although the payment isn't very high, the app itself is so simple and won't bog your phone down, so it's still worth mentioning and recommending. The best part of this app is their program for referring friends. There are also some surveys included for earning more.

## Data Wallet:

This app functions by giving you money to gather information about the way you use and browse social media platforms. You may only use this on iOS devices, so keep that in mind.

## Sweat Coin:

This app is very new compared to the others in this chapter, but Sweat Coin gives you money for walking and allowing them to keep track of the places you are going. You will earn credits that allow you to redeem the points for items like charger adapters or sunglasses. This isn't exactly passive income, but you could sell the items to make some extra money.

## Conclusion on Passive Income Apps:

As mentioned, none of the applications above are going to make you rich on their own. However, these apps will help you a lot with your passive income goals. Use as many apps as you possibly can to increase your profits and don't forget to look for more outside of the ones listed in this book.

# Chapter 4
# Lead Capture Websites, Idea Licensing,
# and More

You can be on your way to earning over $1000 each month using this next idea. Think about a content site that is Google-friendly that has a high conversion inquiry for gathering details (including possibly a free report). Or think about bolder websites such as directory websites that have local lawyers or plumbers, for example.

## Passive Income Strategy #10: Lead Capture Sites.

Leads' contact details aid local businesses in bringing in countless extra clients annually. In other words, you can earn money on the information you gather and then sell to other sources. Think of the example of making a website for individuals seeking storage and then selling customer leads to a company that does local storage. This is called the model of the Internet Landlord. Consider the companies out there who consider a new client worth thousands of dollars, including realtors, surgeons, dentists, accountants, and more. Search for lead capture websites to get started with this.

## Passive Income Strategy #11: Get an Idea Licensed.

Not everyone needs to be a guru of products to get an idea licensed by a business. The process for making this into a passive income stream is long and drawn out, but it will pay off if you do it right! You can take products to manufacturers of equipment and conferences to have them reach big businesses, such as Coca-Cola. Another idea is selling an idea to a network or reality TV producer. Websites such as Virtual Pitchfest allow you to place your pitch into the clutches of important decision makers, and you will always get an answer.

Although certain networks will ask for an idea that's already finished and comes with talent, some networks are only seeking new, fresh ideas and are more than willing to give the idea owners money for them. In some cases, the networks might give you some credit for helping development.

## More Passive Income Ideas:

Most people who are interested in the idea of passive income have at least heard of drop shipping. This also applies to those who have dabbled in or researched the world of online business. But what does the term drop shipping really mean? Why is this becoming a term that is more and more popular? And how can you use it to help your existing business grow? In the next section, we are going to dedicate the entire chapter to covering this, including:

- What drop shipping really is.

- The benefits of this business model.

- How you can find drop shippers.

- How to choose the right drop shipper for passive income.

- How you can integrate a drop shipper with your store.

You can learn to become a drop shipper yourself or just use one to make your business better. If this sounds interesting to you as a passive income seeker, keep reading to learn more!

# Chapter 5
# Your Guide to Passive Income from Drop Shipping

What exactly does the term "drop shipping" refer to? Drop shipping is essentially a method of shipping items to clients from a vendor or third party supply source, without the need for an in between step, such as storing the products in a physical place. Here is how a typical company would do things without using drop shipping:

- The company will routinely order items from a manufacturer to keep a certain amount of the inventory around to sell.

- The company keeps the items around until a client specifically orders them.

- The order gets processed individually, then packaged and shipped to the client. This work would be done by you.

However, when you are using a drop shipper, the process is not the same. It involves the customer ordering items from your company, you passing the information about the order to the drop shipper, and then that drop shipper packaging the items and sending them to your client.

## Passive Income Strategy #12: Using Drop Shipping.

Your next question probably involves the benefits of using this method as opposed to the more commonly used method first mentioned. With drop shipping, you don't have to keep physical items on hand at all times. This frees your company up in many ways, including monetarily, labor-wise, and time-wise.

- **No Storage Hassle:** Keeping your items on hand costs money, as does maintaining the property for storing them. Even when your company only drop ships a fraction of the merchandise, it can free up resources for your products that require more care and attention. This will even let you offer products that you wouldn't typically be able to send because of your location, like perishable items or very big products. You may base your company anywhere on earth and you can still have your products reach your clients in a timely fashion.

- **Savings**: Another advantage to choosing drop shipping is that the drop shipper will be handling the physical steps of shipping and packaging your products. Since drop shippers are oftentimes bigger companies handling multiple orders each and every day, they might already have some shipping rates negotiated that are a better deal than your medium or small business rates.

In other words, these savings will be transferred to you, benefiting both your customers and your company! In addition, drop shipping may reduce your losses from damaged items with the direct route to customer from the warehouse.

- Preventing Issues with Customer Service: Along with getting rid of the headache of storing physical inventory, drop shipping may eliminate problems with customer service and logistics, in general. You won't have to deal with shortages or overstock, and your business also won't be at risk for the shift trends that make some items suddenly be un-sellable.

If you end up needing to bring new items in, expanding your existing item selection, a lot of drop shippers already offer a big variety of products, from classic seller or niche items. Considering your ability to grow and the ability to select where your business will be based, drop shipping will heighten your company's scalability.

## How to Select a Drop Shipping Source:

If, after reading that section, you are sold on drop shipping, but don't know where to start, we're here to help. The internet is a great place to begin your research, but don't expect it to be as simple as searching for the term drop shipper and finding the best source out there instantly.

## Searching the Right Way:

Many drop shippers work with medium or small companies such as yours and may not show up immediately on Google if they don't have strong SEO. In order to find the best drop shipper, expand the search to have vocabulary like "warehouse," or "bulk" or "reseller." You can also include terms such as "supplier" or "wholesale drop shipping." You may also combine these works with the specific types of items you are wanting to sell with your business. You should be aware of what your niche is called before you try to search since various drop shippers have various industries they specialize in.

## Finding Aggregators:

You may also seek out drop shipper aggregators on the internet, by looking at comparison lists or articles on blogs. You may also look to actual businesses that are formed around the idea of selecting a great drop shipper for specific companies. These may be either paid or free resources, but as with the concept of drop shipping, make sure you do plenty of research so you can choose a reputable, reliable, honest person. You don't need to limit yourself to just looking online, though. Another choice is to get in touch with the specific manufacturer of what you want to sell in a more direct way.

The majority of manufacturers will gladly give you a list of drop shippers who have their items and will also usually give you their thoughts on the matter. You may even end up with a better deal by calling a manufacturer directly. You never know until you try!

## Choosing the Best Drop Shipper:

Once you have gathered a list of drop shipping sources to pick from, how are you to make a good selection? The first thing you must do is have a solid concept of how your company will look, mentally, along with what the process of ordering will be with your drop shipper. Here are some factors to consider:

- **What cost are their goods and what do they offer?** Do they have extra fees, alternative payment options? If that particular drop shipper doesn't match your overhead or desired inventory, your choice is made much easier.

- **Who is their shipping provider?** Do they have a well-known shipping provider who is capable of meeting your needs? Are they able to ship to any area in your specific city or region? Are there limitations for their shipping?

- **Have they been doing this long?** Someone with a lot of experience with drop shipping is preferred, especially if they have safe shipments and happy clients stretching back at least 10 years.

- **Do they ship to others?** You should check if this is the drop shipper your competitors are using. This isn't necessarily bad. If you signed up with them, would you be a smaller client for them or larger? A middle range client is best so your drop shipper won't be leaving their comfort level to serve you.

- **Do they have any customization options?** Are you able to place your logo onto the packaging that goes to the client? Can you put extra contact info or coupon codes? Are there confirmation emails for every order sent? What about a return policy for the customers?

Each question above is helpful to ask, but don't forget to also ask the customers, not just the drop shipper. Look for online reviews, forum discussions, and social media comments, or just ask to see a list of references. Don't forget to make your own decision based on plenty of research.

Choosing to add drop shipping to your business can really transform it in many ways, inching it more toward a passive income stream. And that takes care of our beginner drop shipping guide. There's a lot to benefit from with the versatility and streamlining of drop shipping. If you make sure to stick with the guidelines above, you will have a great store and a quality line of passive income coming in.

# Chapter 6
# Affiliate Links, eBooks, Courses, and More

Many people who are interested in passive income already know about affiliate marketing, but this chapter will cover it in detail just in case you don't.

## Passive Income Strategy #13: Affiliate Marketing.

You can get a good passive income stream going with earning from affiliate marketing. This method can be even easier than repurposing content or writing an e-book, since you only have to create content for a blog and bring traffic to it. Essentially, you make an agreement with a website that sells something and link to it on your blog or book. Each time someone clicks the link on your source, and buys a product, you earn a small commission. Some affiliate sources even pay you per click, so do your research!

The majority of people will find that they can earn a sale with affiliate marketing within just a month of getting their site up and running. And you don't even have to deal with the product itself! Here are some benefits to going this route:

- **Freedom to Choose the Topic:** With affiliate marketing, you can earn money talking about almost any product imaginable, including resources and tools online, people's books, physical items, and more. The fees for affiliate marketing can vary a lot depending on the items you discuss on your blog and try to sell.

- **Finding a Unique Niche:** For affiliate marketing, you will have the best chance if you promote items in areas where there are already affiliate marketers working. People in the niche of small business help already have programs for affiliate marketing in place, including theme makers for WordPress, hosting providers, and online course instructors. In contrast, trying to sell fitness items would be harder since there won't already be programs to get signed up with or the ones that do exist may be hard to navigate for a beginner.

- **Get Specific:** In order to be successful in this area, it's crucial that your website or blog has a specific focus (like juicing or philosophy books) and that you stick with products that are relevant to that niche specifically. That way, readers who find your blog will find your opinion trustworthy enough to buy from the links. If, on the other hand, you wrote a blog for writing, marketing, and technology, it won't move enough traffic to it to earn you much money. With that being said, make sure the niche you choose has plenty of items to sell (at least 50).

## What are the Best Items to Market?

You will have the best luck with affiliate marketing if you stick with digital items such as online classes or e-books. They lead to higher percentage splits. You can also go for recurring services online, such as gambling or hosting. Another tip you can use to earn a passive income with affiliate marketing is to put links for your affiliate items onto your email or e-books. This allows your website to look more genuine to Google and your audience is more likely to go for links that they find in trustworthy and enjoyable sources.

## Passive Income Strategy #14: Writing and Selling e-Books.

This model is very popular for content creators and bloggers because it's fairly easy to write a book and sell it through online marketing tactics, including online networking, your blog, and guest posting. What you need to watch out for is how you price the book. Be wary of niches that have an audience who doesn't want to pay over $5 for their book. You can repackage your book to sell it in places such as Amazon, where plenty of traffic goes.

- **Pricing**: If you do go this route, try to put your book at less than $10 since this is typically the highest pricing point. It also lets you gain a larger percentage according to the rules of Amazon. The ones who do end up buying the book through Amazon usually wouldn't have found it in other places, so you won't be losing out on profit.

- **Asking People to Affiliate Market for You:** The best way to earn a profit on your e-book is by getting email marketers or bloggers to affiliate market it for you. You can talk to affiliates individually or list your books on sits such as Click Bank.

- **Hire an e-book Service**: Not everyone is a great writer, but most of us have ideas. If you are one of these people, you can use a service and hire someone to write your e-book for you. All you need is a vision!

## Passive Income Strategy #15: Selling Memberships and Courses.

This is referring to multimedia-driven and members-only sites and it takes quite a bit of work. This is a passive income stream idea for someone who isn't afraid of getting their hands dirty and putting their nose to the grindstone before seeing the benefits pay off. For a course you can write hundreds of thousands of words, hours and hours of audio and video, and templates and checklists to go with these resources. But you can earn great money this way.

### What is Your Niche?

Figure out what your niche is; a subject you know like the back of your hand. If this applies to you, creating a course for it is the best way to earn passive income. It will require five times longer than it takes to make an e-book, but you will be able to charge much more money for it. You can take this to the next level by charging a monthly cost for new resources, updates, forums, direct answers to questions, personal coaching, and more. After all, this is a method for getting passive income, and that's what we all want here.

### How to Create the Site:

You can create a whole members-only site for whatever your niche is with WordPress and a site called Wishlist member. This requires just a couple weeks and really isn't hard at all. One huge tip you should consider is that you can earn great money with a topic that doesn't get a lot of traffic if it's a very specific niche.

Unlike other methods for earning passive income, you may earn money by instructing people on a niched, specific topic. Anything from breeding a certain type of dog to juice fasting can be done.

## Finding the Right Market:

Your first question in regards to this is probably what you should make a course about. You need to find the right market, meaning a market that has demand. The best way to find out the level of demand for a topic is to find out who is searching for it and see if they will pay money to get information on it. One way to seek out new topics for courses is to use Long Tail Pro. This helps you discover niches that there aren't many others in yet, but still get plenty of online searches. This is a must to know about since most topics are already saturated and way too competitive to succeed in.

## Will People Buy?

To find out whether people are going to want to buy your class, you can create pages on LeadPages. You can also use LeadPages to find out the best prices to put on your class or course. This will show you how profitable your idea is and how much you can charge.

# Chapter 7
# Comparing Products and Static Sites

Too many people waste their lives commuting to a job they hate and waiting for the day to be over, just so they can go home, go to bed, and repeat the whole process the next day. Your life is too short to live waiting for the weekend! Take action now and create the passive income streams that will make living a free life possible. Here are some more ideas.

## Passive Income Strategy #16: Compare Products.

Did you know that you can earn money comparing products that already exist? To do this, look for a niche that has a lot of products in it. They must all have pretty complex mixes of features. In other words, the items must have features that make customers wonder how to choose what to buy. Then, follow these steps:

- **Make a Site:** Create a website that shares useful information and content, like how-to blogs, tutorials, and more, in this niche. Next, you need to review the services and products in this niche (including the pros and cons). If you may combine all of this into text that includes photos, that's helpful.

- **Comparison Table:** In addition, you should make a comparison table that lists each product and rates it side by side considering its features. This will help customers choose which item is best for them by looking at all of the information. For each item, there will be a purchase link page to a seller (on Amazon or another source). These are the affiliate links.

- **Find Something You Like:** If you're going to create a site like this, try to make it something you actually care about, otherwise it won't be easy to stick with it. Plus, people reading will be a lot likelier to trust and enjoy your writing if you are enthusiastic about what you're saying and sound sincere.

This passive income stream idea is similar to the idea of creating review sites, but combined with Amazon affiliate marketing.

## Passive Income Strategy #17: Google AdSense.

Did you know that you can earn a passive income using Google AdSense and static sites? For this, you have to think very specifically. This doesn't involve writing about cats and then putting Google AdSense in the writing. Instead, think about making one comprehensive, complete guide-focused site for a highly specific niche subject (like a bed and breakfast businesses in Duluth Michigan). The more specific you can get the better. Next, you will go look for businesses that would want to purchase ad space on the website as soon as you have a dedicated following of readers.

- **Space for Guest Posting:** When most people think about ads, they picture banners, but these are not successful for converting audience members to click through. A much better method is selling space for guest posting (including giving advertisers the chance to write a valuable article for the blog). You can also sell text links in your articles. Next, you can look into widget ads.

- **Widget Ads:** How do widget ads work? Think of a blog that's all about traveling. You could ad a widget for Expedia booking, along with a widget for a travel insurance company instead of placing a typical boring ad banner. This method is great because your audience members can begin to buy directly from your website's sidebar, which switches the transaction to the advertiser's website when necessary.

This idea can earn you money if you know how to bring plenty of traffic to the website. If you want to take it a step further and raise your chance of success, you can set up many of these websites and be on your way to earning a large income in just a year. If you're interested in this idea, make sure you research ways to get more traffic to your blog or website.

## Passive Income Strategy #18: More Apps for Passive Income.

Another method for earning passive income is to use investment advisor applications that will invest your extra change for you. The apps included in this section are all investment advice applications. They do cost a small amount of money to set up, usually (about $5, on average) and instantly take your money and give you advice about how to use this money. These apps are great because they give you a bonus to help you begin with investing and the trades are free from commissions!

## Apps for Investment Help:

Keep in mind that you don't have to deposit a lot, but you have a higher chance to earn more money if you put more in. These applications are perfect for those who have been meaning to learn about investing and want a resource for that. Each application listed will invest the money into ETFs (exchange traded funds), which are securities that function as a stock group and aren't as risky as purchasing one stock on its own. Another great thing about these apps is that you can quit them whenever you want and remove your bank account from them. Let's look at them now.

## Acorns Application:

This app is like other investing apps but doesn't let you pick your own ETFs. Rather, you are given a choice of five levels of risk, ranging from aggressive to conservative amounts of risk.

- **Aggressive Investing:** Young investors usually are suggested to go with the more aggressive style of investing, as long as they don't already have a lot of debt. If you are seeking an application that will take care of 100 percent of the process of investing, this is where you should begin.

- **The Spare Change Function:** Some find the best part of this application to be the option for using your spare change. If you hook up your credit card to the application account, every time you buy something, your card will round up your buy to the nearest amount. That spare change will be put into the Acorns account to be invested. The application requires you to pay a dollar each month, but if you're a college student, you're exempt from paying for four years. You need an EDU address to prove that you're actually a student. You may also refer friends and receive bonuses.

## Stash Invest Application:

This application takes your age and financial information, then gives you ideas for what to purchase depending on the level of risk you prefer to take. This is different from other investment apps since it allows you to invest in that which you are interested in. For instance, if you care a lot about solar power, the app will bring up a couple recommendations for you to look at. Some of these will come with dividends, so that you will get money for being invested. This can turn into bonuses every few months.

In addition, there's an educational section included for those who want to learn about investing and the stock market. Although registration is free, if you have more than $5,000 invested with Stash, you need to pay a dollar per month or .025 percent of the investment amount. You can earn more money by getting your friends to sign up with a referral link.

## The Clink Application:

This app is a little different than the previous ones listed. Clink will ask you to invest a dollar each day, which can be withdrawn automatically from your bank account. In addition, it allows you to choose how much of your spending to invest. For instance, if you bought a meal for $10 and wish to invest 10 percent, $1 will be invested. Registration for Clink is completely free, but you will be charged a dollar a month to use the app.

## Apps that Pay for Screen Unlocking:

The apps in this part of the book will give you money for unlocking your phone's screen. As soon as you install the apps, you will see an advertisement that appears every time you go to unlock the phone. You will be paid to disengage or engage with this advertisement. The income is considered passive since you are not doing anything that you wouldn't usually do.

You won't receive money every time you unlock the phone. Each of these applications uses a different type of algorithm, so it's hard to say when you will get money for unlocking the device. Remember that these apps can be used simultaneously, but you will need to swipe more times than usual to get through them.

## The SlideJoy Application:

As soon as you sign up with this app, you will get a bonus of 20 cents in the account only for registration. As soon as your phone locks like usually, just swipe left in order to find out more about this advertisement, or slide right in order to get to your phone's home screen. Whichever direction you choose to swipe, you will still earn money. In other words, you get paid whether or not you engage with the advertisement. You have to have made at least a dollar in order to cash out to Google Play, PayPal, or Square Cash. You may also give this money to a charity. One of the best parts about this app, however, is that they have a great referral program that allows you to earn 20 percent of what your friends earn on it forever.

## The Adme App:

This one is similar to the one above in that it pays you whether or not you choose to engage with their advertisement on your phone screen. You will receive a bonus of one dollar for signing up and can get your cash as soon as you earn at least $10 with the app. You may only redeem this cash if you have a PayPal account that has been verified. You may also earn extra money if you refer friends to the program and for every friend you will get a 50 cent bonus.

## The Whaff Locker App:

This app offers you a bonus when you register with a code (BQ17928). Every time you unlock your screen, the app will pay you 3 cents. But there is a cap on the amount you can earn within a day so don't try to unlock your screen over and over to earn more.

## The Fronto App:

This add appears to be the best in terms of what they pay you. Some people say they make just $5 each month but others say they earn $20. Just try saving up until your balance gets up to $25 so that your points stretch further when you use this app. The difference with this ad is the fact that you make more money if you do engage with the advertisements on your phone, but even if you don't, you will still earn some money.

## FAQ for Passive Income Applications:

There are probably a lot of different questions about the way these applications function, so this section will focus on answering those. This will allow you to make a more informed decision about whether or not to download one or more of these apps onto your phone. Here are the questions.

- **Will your information be protected?** Your information should always be safe and private. Each of the applications listed above use your data anonymously and in an encrypted format. To put it another way, there isn't any way to trade the data back to you personally, so it stays private.

- **Why won't this app work for me?** Some users might come across a problem where the app doesn't function on their phone or tablet. If this does happen for you, your OS may be out of date or you might need to update the device.

- **How do these apps pay you?** When you allow these apps to gather information from your device or phone, they sell this info as marketing research, which is considered very valuable. This information is then used by businesses to make their services and products better for us as the consumers.

## Passive Income Strategy #19: Make a Subscription Business.

This is another passive income strategy that requires hard work upfront, like most of the others. However, if you do it right, you can rest and allow the work to do itself. As soon as you have come up with your product and concept, you can hire a fulfillment business to send and package your products or subscription products, so you don't have to. Cratejoy is there to take care of signing new clients up and managing other processes, leaving you free to enjoy your passive income.

## What are Subscription Boxes?

These are the ideal way to get shopping done. They give consumers access to new brands, offer unique experiences for shopping, and make the process of checking your mail into something enjoyable rather than tedious. On the other hand, they will give you a model for stable finances and can bring in monthly revenue for just about any niche out there, from pets, to beauty, to puzzle enthusiasts. If there is already a community for the category or product on the internet, you can probably start a subscription box related to it. The best tip to follow is that the more unique the niche is, the better you will do.

## Find Your Market:

The best way to start a business is to begin with a great idea. And for subscription box companies specifically, the more specific you are, the more successful you will be. You can think of a niche as a specific, small market for services and products. One simple way to consider this as it relates to a subscription box company is to think about what your box would have inside of it. Consider which products would be a part of it, how they are unique, and how these traits represent your box's values.

Thinking on these questions matters because the more specific you are in the niche, the simpler it will be to tailor and curate the products to your specific audience members, allowing you to gain retention and make an amazing customer service experience. In addition, marketing isn't as hard if you know how to zoom in on your audience and understand who is buying from you, which brings me to the next point.

## Find Out Who Your Customers Are:

The next step is to do some research into your potential clients. Who are these people and what are their habits of shopping like? Odds are, once you've already gone through the first step, you already have an idea of who will be purchasing your product or box. Then you need to get even more specific with it. For this step, your goal should be to create an assumption that is realistic about your client, mostly through polling, competitive analysis, and data. Here's how:

- Find resources for your niche's market analysis information.

- Who are your competitors serving in your specific niche?

- Poll your family and friends, or use online polls.

Once you have already researched your potential customers, come up with a more specific profile for them. List the habits they will have in terms of shopping, how much they earn each year, their hobbies and interests, their reasons for purchasing, sensitivities, and more. Get as detailed as possible for defining the clients.

## Create your Prototype:

The next step involves creating your prototype box. This is just another way to say your earliest model product. This will allow you to create a foundation for the experience of your future customers. Here are some considerations you must take as a new owner of a subscription box company:

- How big do you want your box to be? (This is important because it will affect shipping costs for you).

- How many objects are you going to place in the box every month?

- Are the products safe to ship or will you need to buy special materials to pack it?

- Do you need to include printed materials in the box?

- How will the aesthetic and design be for your box? Is there a presentation style that your audience will like best?

- Is your product an experience instead of just products? Does it stand out?

Ensure that your box is priced at a reasonable number that your clients can afford to pay, but is high enough to earn you a decent amount of money. Don't forget to change this as you go and let the idea evolve. If you really stick with this, you should have a fair amount of passive income coming in within a short time.

## Passive Income Strategy #20: Sell Outsourced Skills.

You can earn money selling your own outsourced skills and services to businesses or people who need them. This can include anything from copy writing, to graphic design, or even receptionist duties. Here is what you need to do for this:

## Make a Website Selling Your Skill:

Create a website and use SEO research to make it appear in search results. The website must be very easy to use so that the person using it doesn't have any difficulties or questions that hold them back. This can allow them to submit an order and pay right away using PayPal. Price the service you are selling at some kind of premium so you can earn good profits. Ensure that your order form is very simple and clear, displayed in an easy to find area on your website, with a simple way to pay for your customers.

## How is this Passive?

This process can be passive for certain skills, as long as you make an agreement that you will receive a percentage of profits earned from your work. For instance, if you get hired to design a logo for a website, you should get a certain percentage of that website's profits for your work. Keep in mind that this doesn't always work, so you have to set up the agreement beforehand.

## Use Freelance Websites:

Alternatively, you may sign up for sources that connect freelancers with people seeking to hire those with skills. This is not as passive as other sources of income, but can require only small amounts of work to get paid if you find the right sources and build up your references.

## In Summary:

As you can see, there are countless ways for you to earn passive income online from home. There's no reason that you have to stay involved in the rat race. Instead, you can stay at home and spend more time with your spouse or kids by working hard now and watching the cash roll in later.

# Conclusion

Thanks for reading *15+ Proven Income Strategies to Earn You $1000+ a Month in 60 Days or Less.*

Hopefully this extensive guide has supplied you with at least a few ideas you can put to work to start earning passive income now. If you work hard, you can have a passive income stream within 60 days or less!

Good luck with your passive income plan and thanks again for reading!

www.ingramcontent.com/pod-product-compliance
Lightning Source LLC
Chambersburg PA
CBHW071231220526
45468CB00002B/801